W9-DDK-176

SWAYING STRINGS

By KAREN LATCHANA KENNEY

Illustrated by JOSHUA HEINSZ

Music by MARK OBLINGER

CANTATA
LEARNING

WWW.CANTATALEARNING.COM

CANTATA LEARNING

Published by Cantata Learning
1710 Roe Crest Drive
North Mankato, MN 56003
www.cantatalearning.com

Library of Congress Cataloging-in-Publication Data

Names: Kenney, Karen Latchana, author. | Heinsz, Joshua, illustrator. |
    Oblinger, Mark, composer.
Title: Swaying strings / by Karen Latchana Kenney ; illustrated by Joshua
    Heinsz ; music by Mark Oblinger.
Description: North Mankato, MN : Cantata Learning, [2019] | Series: The
    physics of music | Includes bibliographical references.
Identifiers: LCCN 2018026089 (print) | LCCN 2018027209 (ebook) | ISBN
    9781684103645 (eBook) | ISBN 9781684103447 (hardcover)
Subjects: LCSH: Stringed instruments--Juvenile literature. | Children's
    songs, English.
Classification: LCC ML750 (ebook) | LCC ML750 .K46 2019 (print) | DDC
    787--dc23
LC record available at https://lccn.loc.gov/2018026089

Book design and art direction: Tim Palin Creative
Editorial direction: Kellie M. Hultgren
Music direction: Elizabeth Draper
Music arranged and produced by Mark Oblinger

Printed in the United States of America.
0397

ACCESS THE MUSIC!

SCAN CODE WITH MOBILE APP

CANTATALEARNING.COM

TIPS TO SUPPORT LITERACY AT HOME

WHY READING AND SINGING WITH YOUR CHILD IS SO IMPORTANT

Daily reading with your child leads to increased academic achievement. Music and songs, specifically rhyming songs, are a fun and easy way to build early literacy and language development. Music skills correlate significantly with both phonological awareness and reading development. Singing helps build vocabulary and speech development. And reading and appreciating music together is a wonderful way to strengthen your relationship.

READ AND SING EVERY DAY!

TIPS FOR USING CANTATA LEARNING BOOKS AND SONGS DURING YOUR DAILY STORY TIME

1. As you sing and read, point out the different words on the page that rhyme. Suggest other words that rhyme.

2. Memorize simple rhymes such as Itsy Bitsy Spider and sing them together. This encourages comprehension skills and early literacy skills.

3. Use the questions in the back of each book to guide your singing and storytelling.

4. Read the included sheet music with your child while you listen to the song. How do the music notes correlate to the words of the song?

5. Sing along on the go and at home. Access music by scanning the QR code on each Cantata book. You can also stream or download the music for free to your computer, smartphone, or mobile device.

Devoting time to daily reading shows that you are available for your child. Together, you are building language, literacy, and listening skills.

Have fun reading and singing!

How do you play **stringed instruments**? You can pluck, pick, or strum strings. You can also pull a bow across them.

Playing strings makes them **vibrate** back and forth. The moving strings make the air vibrate, too. These moving vibrations are called **waves**. When the waves reach your ears, you hear the instrument's sound.

Are you ready to make some sound waves? Turn the page and sing along!

You can make strings sing in all kinds of ways!
Run your fingers over four on the ukulele.

Notes grow in the body from those gentle strums.
Sing of hope and rainbows as the **rhythm** hums.

With just a little strum, you'll hear that *brrriiiinnngg*!
That sweet sound's made by vibrating strings.

They move back and forth, pushing the air,
sending waves of notes from here to there.

From low to high, change the **pitch** as you pick.
Press on the strings. Yes, that's the trick!

Faster vibrations come from shorter strings.
The notes climb higher, *da-da-ding-ding-ding*.

With just a little strum, you'll hear that *brrriiiinnngg*! That sweet sound's made by vibrating strings.

They move back and forth, pushing the air, sending waves of notes from here to there.

From thick to thin cello strings are arranged.
Draw a bow across to hear the instrument's range.

Thick strings move slow, sounding low and deep.
Thin strings sound high with bigger **frequencies**.

With just a little strum, you'll hear that *brrriiiinnngg*!
That sweet sound's made by vibrating strings.

They move back and forth, pushing the air,
sending waves of notes from here to there.

The piano keys tinkle. Play that jazzy tune over deep bass beats, *da-da-dou, dou, dou.*

Pressing the keys lets the hammers fly, striking blue sounds from the strings inside.

With just a little strum, you'll hear that *brrriiiinnngg*!
That sweet sound's made by vibrating strings.

They move back and forth, pushing the air,
sending waves of notes from here to there.

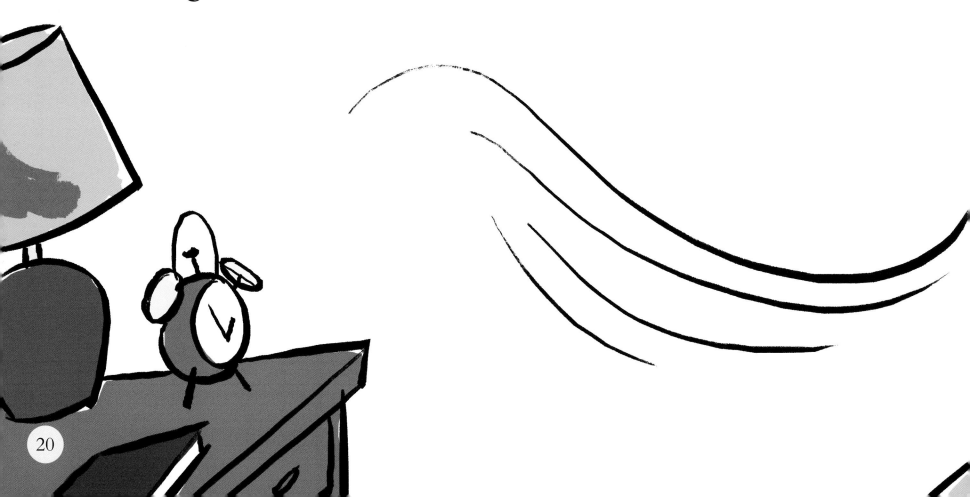

SONG LYRICS
Swaying Strings

You can make strings sing in all kinds of ways!
Run your fingers over four on the ukulele.
Notes grow in the body from those gentle strums.
Sing of hope and rainbows as the rhythm hums.

With just a little strum, you'll hear that
   brrriiiinnngg!
That sweet sound's made by vibrating strings.
They move back and forth, pushing the air,
sending waves of notes from here to there.

From low to high, change the pitch as you pick.
Press on the strings. Yes, that's the trick!
Faster vibrations come from shorter strings.
The notes climb higher, *da-da-ding-ding-ding.*

With just a little strum, you'll hear that
   brrriiiinnngg!
That sweet sound's made by vibrating strings.
They move back and forth, pushing the air,
sending waves of notes from here to there.

From thick to thin cello strings are arranged.
Draw a bow across to hear the instrument's
   range.

Thick strings move slow, sounding low and deep.
Thin strings sound high with bigger frequencies.

With just a little strum, you'll hear that
   brrriiiinnngg!
That sweet sound's made by vibrating strings.
They move back and forth, pushing the air,
sending waves of notes from here to there.

The piano keys tinkle. Play that jazzy tune
over deep bass beats, *da-da-dou, dou, dou.*
Pressing the keys lets the hammers fly,
striking blue sounds from the strings inside.

With just a little strum, you'll hear that
   brrriiiinnngg!
That sweet sound's made by vibrating strings.
They move back and forth, pushing the air,
sending waves of notes from here to there.

Swaying Strings

World
Mark Oblinger

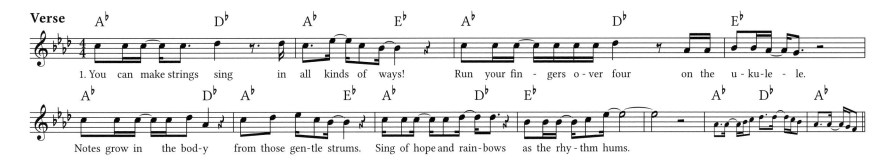

Verse

1. You can make strings sing in all kinds of ways! Run your fin - gers o - ver four on the u - ku - le - le.

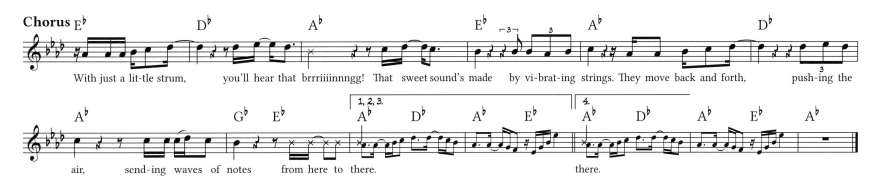

Notes grow in the bod-y from those gen-tle strums. Sing of hope and rain-bows as the rhy - thm hums.

Chorus

With just a lit-tle strum, you'll hear that brrriiiinnngg! That sweet sound's made by vi-brat-ing strings. They move back and forth, push-ing the

air, send-ing waves of notes from here to there. there.

Verse 2
From low to high, change the pitch as you pick.
Press on the strings. Yes, that's the trick!
Faster vibrations come from shorter strings.
The notes climb higher, da-da-ding-ding-ding.

Chorus

Verse 3
From thick to thin cello strings are arranged.
Draw a bow across to hear the instrument's range.
Thick strings move slow, sounding low and deep.
Thin strings sound high with bigger frequencies.

Chorus

Verse 4
The piano keys tinkle. Play that jazzy tune
over deep bass beats, da-da-dou dou dou.
Pressing the keys lets the hammers fly,
striking blue sounds from the strings inside.

Chorus

GLOSSARY

frequencies—number of vibrations per second in a sound wave

pitch—how high or low a musical note sounds

rhythm—a sound pattern

stringed instruments—instruments with strings that vibrate to make sound

vibrate—to quickly move back and forth

waves—movements of vibrating air that carry sound

CRITICAL THINKING QUESTIONS

1. Stringed instruments are played in different ways to make different sounds. Listen to recordings of banjo and violin music. Players use picks on the banjo and a bow for the violin. Try to describe their different sounds.

2. Look at the ukulele on pages 6–7 and the guitarrón on pages 12–13. How are these two stringed instruments the same? How are they different?

3. Listen to the song and act out the chorus. Some of the kids in your class can be the strings in a center circle. Some can be the air in outer circles. Make a gentle sound wave by bumping into each other from the strings to the air.

TO LEARN MORE

Chris Barton. *88 Instruments*. New York: Alfred A. Knopf, 2016.

Johnson, Robin. *How Does Sound Change?* New York: Crabtree, 2014.

Kenney, Karen Latchana. *Striking Sounds.* North Mankato, MN: Cantata Learning, 2019.

Nunn, Daniel. *Strings*. Chicago: Heinemann, 2012.